73514
Rose

F
9
.R6

D1506469

J.M.R.

Here on this thin high earth old stones lean in the wind. Townwards, gray shingled roofs and a fine church tower are intermassed with the green crowns of old trees. Below the hill near Peach's Point it is said that the first white settler made his home in a hogshead on the beach. Later, came fisher folk from the Channel Islands and west of England

Christmas 1943

Ruth,
from Dorothy

NORTHEAST FROM BOSTON

by Jack Manley Rosé

WILLIAMSBURG TODAY & YESTERDAY

NORTHEAST FROM BOSTON

LONG WHARF, BOSTON. From this old wharf stretching far out
into the harbor as early as 1710, the British were evacuated in 1776.

Northeast from Boston

BY JACK MANLEY ROSÉ

CAPTIONS BY GRACE NORTON ROSÉ

73514

NEW YORK · G. P. PUTNAM'S SONS · MCMXXXXI

COPYRIGHT, 1941, BY JACK MANLEY ROSÉ

*All rights reserved. This book, or parts thereof,
must not be reproduced in any form without permission*

Typography by Robert Josephy

MANUFACTURED IN U. S. A.

ONTBONNE LIBRARY

Folio
F
9
.R6
1941

ACKNOWLEDGMENTS: *The authors gratefully acknowledge the generous assistance of the following: Miss Dorothy Vaughan, Public Library, Portsmouth, N. H.; Mr. Frank D. Butler, President of the Portsmouth Historical Society, Portsmouth, N. H.; The Cape Ann Scientific Literary and Historical Association, Gloucester, Mass.; The Rockport Historical Society, Rockport, Mass.; The Essex Institute, Salem, Mass.; The Board of Park Commissioners, Salem, Mass.; Miss Caroline O. Emmerton, Salem, Mass.; The Marblehead Historical Society, Marblehead, Mass.; Mr. Henry S. Baldwin, President of the Swampscott Historical Society, Swampscott, Mass.; and The Socony-Vacuum Oil Company for the use of color plates.*

COLOR PLATES

FOREWORD

HEADING "Down East" from Boston is strictly in line with one's inclination and the general trend. For everyone should make this pilgrimage at least every three or four years, if only to see if Old New England can still be found. But Boston Town induces one to linger. It is still amazing to encounter on every street corner citizens who know the city's historic past as they know the incidents in their own lives. Even in casually passing through this town, that endearing quality of an old seaport is evident and unmistakable. So it is fitting to tarry here long enough to make drawings of the present waterfront, at least as much of it as can be glimpsed along what is now Atlantic Avenue and approximately the location of the "Barricado."

The old wharves, rich in history and still in use with the exception of Hancock's and Griffin's, abut upon what was once this "Barricado," built in 1673 across the head of Great Cove to link up the town's defenses. This was a wall or wharf of timber and stones with openings at intervals to let ships pass through to the "Inner Wharves," before the Cove was filled in. Erected to increase wharfage facilities and to protect the town from "fire ships" that might possibly be sent by the French, this "Barricado" came to be known as the "Out Wharves." This is the general line of the present old wharves that are still serving Boston: Long, T, Central, India, and Rowe's.

The little old State House, dating back to British Colonial use, stands in its own square near the waterfront, and is unbelievably impressive. During a lapse in the execution of civic conscience, Boston nearly lost this eighteenth-century architectural relic of Colonial times to the city of Chicago. Only a strenuous effort on the part of public-minded citizens saved it for Massachusetts. When the new Bullfinch-designed State House was completed in 1798, the carved and gilded model of the Sacred Cod, symbol of Boston's financial prosperity, was formally removed and installed in its new quarters.

Near by, and still in the vicinity of the waterfront, are other places famed in legend and history, among them Faneuil Hall, the Cradle of Liberty, the spot (now dry land) where the Tea Party was enacted, and the site of the Boston Massacre. Alongshore, across the Charles River, is the Navy Yard in Charlestown, and on the far bank of the Mystic, once a fur-trading station, is Chelsea, where the Naval Hospital commands the river mouth and a good part of Boston Harbor. Running out of Chelsea and through Revere is the coastwise route that leads "Down East."

And it is in following this route, beyond those wide public beaches with which Boston and its vicinity are so especially blessed, that the "stern and rockbound coast" of northern Massachusetts becomes manifest. The rocky promontory of Nahant, that salty playground of the descendants of the ship-owning and mercantile families of old Boston, looms out beyond the busy chimneys of Lynn.

Northeast of Nahant is Swampscott of dory-building fame, now given over to a concrete sea front of pavilions and parkways. Its historic past is forever linked to the early days of the Massachusetts Bay Colony. At least one fine old house, once owned by John Humphrey and his wife, Lady Susan, daughter of the Earl of Lincoln, and shortly after by the indomitable Lady Deborah Moody, is preserved.

Inland, legendary names may beckon, but Marblehead on the coast is rich in ancient tales of the sea and has still the picturesque quality of other times that appeals to the artist. In fact so full of charm are its crooked little climbing lanes, its rocky ledges, and its fine old houses looking seaward, that to leave this town is difficult indeed.

A rough, weathered, and lonely promontory this rocky bit of land must have been in the days when daring fisherfolk from the Channel Islands and the west coast of England came to settle here in 1633 and call it Marble Harbor. Little elegance and good living obtained in those first hard decades. The people were known for almost a century as a rough, illiterate race.

"Very crasey!" young Captain Goelet of New York, touring this coast in 1750, dubbed this picturesque, straggling cluster of fishing huts on the beaches and the few better homes clinging to the rocky ledges. Even today the crooked streets keep somewhat the character and feeling that it must have had in the eighteenth century.

Drunkenness, fighting, and gambling had ushered in that century, with liquor flowing freely at "Washing Out Day" and even at times at Town

Meeting. Marblehead came to be known as the Smuggling Port for Boston. A peculiar, clipped-off, but broad-voweled dialect persisted among the fisherfolk almost to this day. Recordings of it were made a few years ago and the results published by the Columbia University Press.

Marblehead men in the Revolution gave a good account of themselves. It was their "Amphibious Regiment" under General Glover that helped evacuate Long Island and that ferried George Washington across the Delaware in their whaleboats on that historic Christmas night. Although Marblehead had accumulated some wealth in the fisheries and in foreign trade, the Embargo and the War of 1812 were as ruinous to its commerce as they were to other New England seafaring communities.

But Marblehead now lives by its yachting supremacy and its summer population. It has come to be known as the yachting capital of the eastern seaboard.

Just to the north around Naugus Head is Salem, old and storied. Some dark-browed saltbox houses of the seventeenth century, many four-square white residences of the eighteenth, and at least one whole street of Federal architecture of the very early nineteenth still survive. Salem has had its day of glory, its day of exploitation, its day of depression, and also the usual but more than usually devastating fire. But hope for the preservation of the day of its glory in such monuments as still exist is ever present in the hearts of those who love it. Already the restoration of part of what was once the teeming waterfront has been undertaken by the Federal Government. Salem's motto, "The Wealth of the Indies to the Uttermost Gulf," so true in the years of trade with the Orient, may mean little today as one looks in vain for ghosts of the fine shipping that once crowded its wharves, but particularly in its museums and in its old homes is this motto well preserved.

From Beverly on, the North Shore becomes exceedingly well groomed and fashionable. Pride's Crossing, Beverly Farms, Manchester, and Magnolia have costly homes surmounting the rocky cliffs and dominating the beaches. They stretch up the coast with small but sporting harbor facilities until Gloucester is reached.

Here indeed is a magnificent anchorage and wharfage for the greatest fishing fleet that this country can boast. Here is a town forever concerned with the catch, the sea's dangers, and the homecoming once more. Gloucester was famed as a fine spot for cod fishing before the days when Winslow of the

Plymouth Colony, "in a known place there commonly called Cape Anne," endeavored to establish fishing stages. The right to do so was disputed, and Roger Conant, later one of the "Old Planters" of Salem and then leader of a few honest and industrious men who had settled in this vicinity, acted as peace-maker between the rival factions of the Merchant Adventurers.

Gloucester became known as "The Harbor" in contrast to the more exposed fishing hamlets at Sandy Bay and the other coves of Cape Ann. Today, as yesterday, Gloucester lives by the fishing. The catch in 1905 is said to have been valued at over $3,000,000. The town itself has changed radically, except along the wharves, from a small fishing village to a small modern city. Fires have done what they could to stamp out the treasures of the past. A few streets, particularly Middle Street, have retained some of their past dignity and charm, but it is along the miles of sturdy wharves, approached by water or by land, that the true heart of colorful Gloucester can be found.

From Gloucester all Cape Ann reaches out: a granite island, really, of rare wild beauty and historic interest. Here is the terminal moraine of the Great Glacier. About where it started to recede are the ancient cellar holes of a small village known as Dogtown. It is said that Gloucestermen, when they left on the expedition against Louisburg in 1745, moved their families inland with great dogs to guard them, for fear of an attack on The Harbor by the French fleet.

Sandy Bay, or Rockport as it is now called, on the outer shore and Rocky Neck in East Gloucester have always been the favorite haunts of artists. But the whole Cape is a land of delight, jutting its granite ledges far into the Atlantic and garnering the flood tides, the caressing sea fogs, and the saltiest winds that blow.

Leaving Gloucester one bears northwest by north, for the coastline curves inward from Cape Ann. It is broken by great reaches of marshland, tidewater creeks, and, seaward, by sandy beaches.

Essex, renowned through the centuries for shipbuilding, lies at the head of a small river seemingly hardly wide enough to float a Gloucester schooner down to the sea. But the old yards there are still building Gloucestermen and building them well, although the industry is compelled through an unkind twist of fate to share the roadside with unsightly fried-clam stands and other evidences of the automobile age.

Ipswich, with its long elm-shaded lovely green, and its old stone bridge across the almost depleted river, is also changing rapidly. Beyond it are Rowley and "Ould Newbury," both cherished towns of the past.

"Ould Newbury's" great charm lies in the long stretch of famous High Street, which begins here and runs for six delightful miles through Newburyport parallel with the Merrimac River.

From High Street, after it enters Newburyport, cross streets descend a gentle slope to the river scarcely three or four blocks below. High Street, whose continuous procession of fine homes proclaim the wealth that came from the sea, is the longest stretch of highroad in America still bordered by outstanding examples of the architecture of the late seventeenth to early nineteenth centuries. It may triumphantly survive if civic conscience remains aroused.

It was this street that the rich and eccentric "Lord" Timothy Dexter, that thorn in the flesh of all conservative Newburyporters, offered to pave from one end to the other if only his name might adorn it. It was characteristic of the temper of the town authorities that this offer and other similar offers were refused. After his demise, his fine house and grounds, inappropriately and tastelessly bedizened by wooden statues of his heroes and filigree frippery of one sort or another, resumed the seemly aspect of its neighbors.

Below High Street, toward the river, are houses of antiquity and distinction, and a church or two of importance in the early annals of America. Although bad fires have persistently swept through this colonial town, much remains that is unmistakably associated with the early days of its seafaring and shipbuilding activity. Newburyport lost her grip on ocean supremacy in America after the Revolution, to which she vigorously contributed her share of troops, money, and privateers.

In one of his very charming letters George Washington wrote of this town after a tour of the New England coast: "In visiting the town of Newburyport I have obeyed a favorite inclination and I am much gratified by the indulgence."

The Great Fire of 1811, following Jefferson's Embargo, impoverished the town and ruined the domestic and foreign trade she was beginning to rebuild. "Madison's War," so called by the sailors of Newburyport parading the streets in hungry bands, deriding the tar barrels inverted over the mastheads of idle ships as "Madison's Nightcaps," kept her ships from the sea. Then came a promising revival of shipbuilding under Donald McKay, Currier, and others when the old yards resumed active industry, launching the fast clipper ships of that amazing era before the adoption of steam. But the persistent shoaling up of the river mouth was an inevitable factor in the decline of Newburyport as an important seaport.

Northeast of Newburyport across the Merrimac River and up the coast are Salisbury Beach, Hampton Beach, Great Boar's Head, Little Boar's Head, and the Rye sands. Just inland are old towns that in spite of being on a main highway have a great deal of charm and flavor of the past. But on the coastwise route which the artist follows for natural beauty, the resorts offer more to the summer vacationist than to the seeker of the picturesque relics of the past. There are occasional ocean-edge farms of undoubted antiquity, and many miles of rocky shore interspersed with crescents of rubblestone beach, and now and then a short stretch of wide gray sand. But the mariner must run clear to Portsmouth to find a harbor if caught off these shores in a gale. Hampton River offers some anchorage for those who know the channel, but on the whole it is a forbidding coast of almost primeval ruggedness, its submerged forests and ocean ledges giving evidence of its preglacial origin.

Portsmouth, New Hampshire, reached by the seaward route, takes in Odiorne's Point, where the first settlement in the state was made in 1623, and Newcastle on Great Island. This, a small village of colonial aspect, is given over to old residents, naval officers and their families, and a colony of summer visitors. On the estuary of the Piscataqua River, separating New Hampshire from the State of Maine, is this serenely lovely town of Portsmouth. A grand old seaport of pre-Revolutionary days, it has heartening evidences of survival in its elm-shaded quiet streets and its magnificent old houses of a former epoch. These dignified, three-storied white dwellings, standing close to the street in the English manner, with ample gardens in the rear, speak eloquently of the prosperity and taste of their builders. The placid millponds mirror the shimmering old houses and the white church spires above the tall elms, as does the Piscataqua on calm and windless days of all seasons.

The little city, distinctive and almost unspoiled, delighting not alone the itinerant artist but whoever has the good luck to visit it, is, including Kittery across the river, a fitting climax to a pictorial survey of the shoreline northeast of Boston.

Kittery, in Maine, whose early days as well as later years are closely bound up with the history and spirit of Portsmouth, has a life of its own in its busy

United States Navy Yard and its attendant industries. With the majority of ranking officers living either in Newcastle or Portsmouth, the Yard adds much to the well-being and social charm of the region of the Piscataqua.

So must end the jaunt up this "Down-East" seacoast, through old seaports, along their waterfront clamshell lanes, their wharves and beaches, and their shady commons. With so much pictorial material to tempt the artist's pencil and brush, something that is fine and historic in every town must unfortunately go unrecorded, but the characteristic qualities of each of these harbors of this New England coast are here depicted. They will provide a lasting attraction for all who seek marine enchantment.

G. N. R.

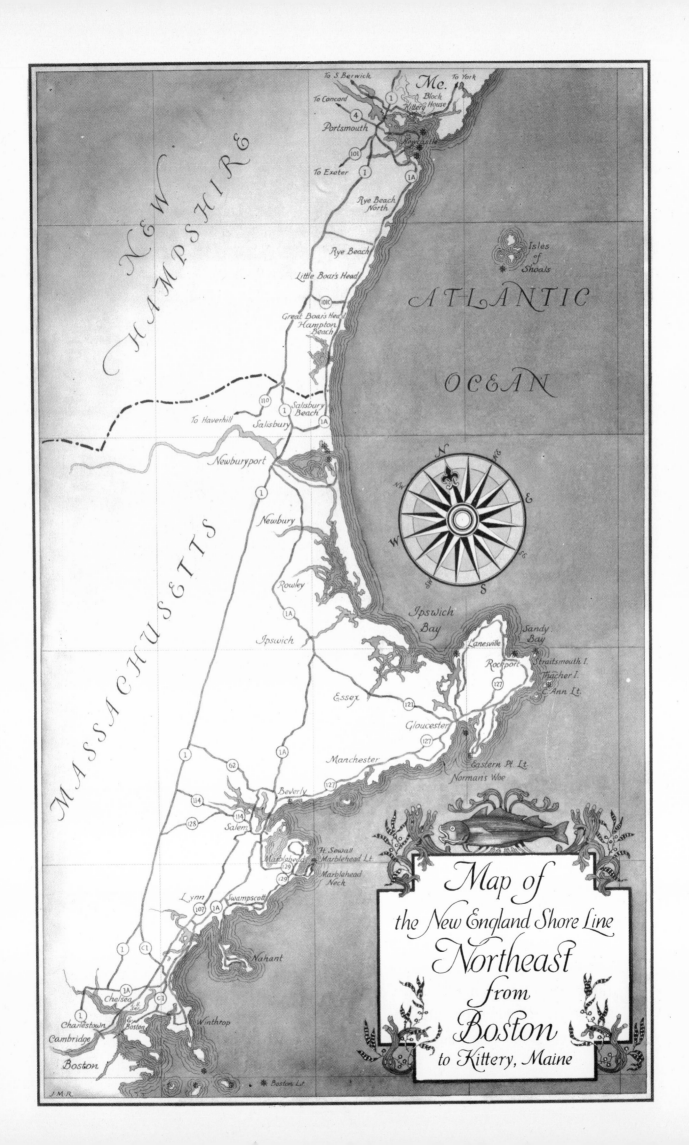

Map of
the New England Shore Line
Northeast
from
Boston
to Kittery, Maine

BOSTON

THE OLD STATE HOUSE. Built and rebuilt after the nine great fires which, in little more than a century, have visited Boston, the present old State House has incorporated in it the outer walls of its predecessor, the Town or Colony House completed in 1713. This was the State House of the British until the Revolution. A huge bonfire was built in front of it when the British yoke was finally thrown off, and the "Bostoneers" took every emblem of royalty and every Tory token and threw them on the flames.

THE CUSTOM HOUSE—OLD AND NEW. The harbor in the early days extended up to the Custom House, built in the style of the Greek revival. The bowsprits of ships at the wharves slanted up across the streets to its very steps. The dome of the old building has been concealed by a towering superstructure serving as a landmark for ships at sea.

BOSTON

T WHARF. Informal in every aspect, this ancient wharf with its long low range of loft buildings is given over to the Bohemian haunts of artists and those whose interests are in seafaring. Gaudily painted Italian or Portuguese fishing boats lie alongside their sleeker sisters, and family parties embark here on Sunday for fishing or yachting. The neck connecting T Wharf with Long Wharf is said to be part of the ancient "Barricado." It is the oldest of the present wharves and was once owned by Andrew Faneuil, the uncle of the more famous Peter, after whom Faneuil Hall was named.

LIGHTSHIP AND LIGHTHOUSE TENDER. Across the Mystic River from Boston is Chelsea, once called Winnisimet, identified with Boston's early history as a fur-trading station and as the northern terminal of what was probably the earliest ferry in North America, subsidized by the General Court of the colony. Here alongshore are the United States Lightship Service Yards, full of colorful interest to the nautical-minded.

NAHANT

ROCKS AT NAHANT. The isthmus of Lynn's public beaches connects the mainland with the rocky headland that is Nahant. Jutting well out to sea, its impregnable and famous cliffs and shallow harbors encircle windswept moors, sweet drowsy hollows, and the shady thoroughfares of a small but fashionable community.

Seldom do the old windjammers from foreign ports come to these harbors now.

HARBOR FROM NAHANT. Lynn has been a center of the shoe industry since two skilled shoemakers from England settled at the location of an earlier settler's tannery, near a clear and rushing stream. Now, the city is an industrial chaos of tenements, stacks, and smoky brick walls of factories and warehouses. Fortunately it is graced seaward by sandy flats and a narrow strip of beautiful public beach stretching out to the rocks of Nahant, and inland by recreational woods and lakes.

THE FISHERMEN'S BEACH. It is said that along this beach in winter frozen cod used to lie stacked like cordwood, and quantities of lobsters could be picked up in summer at low tide. Swampscott was settled in 1629, and was fairly early known as a summer resort for Boston and later famed for the dories built there.

THE TOWN HOUSE. A trifle austere, and withdrawing as well as it can from the motor traffic that winds about it, this storied hall of 1727 has taken part in every important event in the town's history since its erection.

MARBLEHEAD

THE POWDER HOUSE. On a slight rise back of the town is the powder storage place of early wars. Always interesting are these little round structures, but this one has a special appeal in its capping. Built in 1755, it served from the French and Indian Wars through the War of 1812.

JACK MANLEY ROSÉ

OLD POWDER HOUSE
MARBLEHEAD 1755

SHACK ON THE BEACH. From a rough-and-ready fishing hamlet in the Barnegat section on Little Harbor to a community where wealth and security came slowly but surely from the toilsome sea, the port of Marblehead, no longer really important in the fisheries, makes a more certain livelihood now from yachting and the summer visitors.

MARBLEHEAD

WASHINGTON STREET. Adorning Washington Street is this stone church with a fine white tower surmounted by gilded dome. Curving up from the waterfront past the church, this street preserves its air of colonial austerity in the sturdy houses of the eighteenth century that crowd it on each side.

STEPS, ONCE A COWPATH. If ever there was a town that grew up haphazardly and endearingly, that town is Marblehead. It starts at an orderly square surrounded by bland and beautiful early American houses which ignore the red-stone immensity of Abbot Hall in their midst; it curves down into a few unmodern business blocks and innumerable streets, lanes, and crooked byways leading to the harbor.

MARBLEHEAD

THE KING HOOPER HOUSE. Built in 1745 by a young ship owner whose title as "King" was given him by his sailors for the fare he served on shipboard, this house has grandeur combined with simplicity. The ballroom on the third floor, vaulted and beautifully proportioned, serves now as a gallery for the Marblehead Art Association.

THE JEREMIAH LEE MANSION DOORWAY. This fine old monument to the wealth made by New England ship owners before the Revolutionary War is now preserved by the Marblehead Historical Society. The date of its erection is 1768 and the builder, Colonel Jeremiah Lee, that patriotic citizen whose efforts in behalf of the Colonies at the outbreak of hostilities with England are well known.

SALEM

THE PIONEERS' VILLAGE AND THE SHIP ARBELLA. This settlement has been reconstructed for all to see from the humblest dugout of the "Old Planters" to the "Governor's Fayre House." Here is also a representation of the ship *Arbella*, named for that ill-fated Lady Arbella, who with her husband Sir Isaac Johnson sailed in 1630 with Governor John Winthrop's Company, and died very shortly from the privations encountered.

THE PIONEERS' VILLAGE. During the active colonizing years of 1620–1630 along the New England coast, Roger Conant and companions came from their bleak fishing stations on Cape Ann to Naumkeag, a verdant neck of land protected from the northeasters. Here they were joined by Captain John Endicott and a small colony of settlers, and shortly afterwards Salem was laid out just beyond this first settlement.

THE PIERCE-NICHOLS HOUSE. The house itself is a lovely and authentic example of carver McIntyre's work and easily carries one back to the days of Salem's East India trade supremacy.

THE PIERCE-NICHOLS STABLEYARD. Back of the house the stable and carriage house enclose an intimate yard that fully represents the homely everyday life of another century.

SALEM

THE CUSTOM HOUSE. At the head of Derby Wharf, now under reconstruction by the Government, is the Custom House, delightfully Federal in design and built in 1819. It was here that Nathaniel Hawthorne thumbed the ledgers and dreamed the plots of his novels and stories. But almost unsung and sorely needing a bard is the gallant era of the sailing ships that brought fame to Salem in the years just before and after the Revolution.

CHESTNUT STREET, LAID OUT IN 1796.
Cherished through the generations, spared by the devastating fire of 1914, these venerable houses on this
street are Salem's proudest beauty. It is said that no
finer examples of Federal architecture are assembled
in any one American city street than here, where
admirably preserved, quiet, brick and white-painted
façades are dappled by the shadows of old trees.

SALEM

THE HOUSE OF THE SEVEN GABLES. This type of house saw the beginning and end of the witchcraft delusion that, in spite of the liberal teaching and preaching of Roger Williams and Hugh Peters, followed so closely the persecution of the Quakers. Here is the setting of Nathaniel Hawthorne's novel of this name. Intended for and used as a center for settlement work in the neighborhood, this delightful bit of colonial America, situated on the river's edge, now in the summer season dispenses unusual hospitality to the summer tourist.

DOORWAY AND WATER-
FRONT, HOUSE OF THE SEVEN
GABLES. Happily secured to Salem
through the generosity of Miss Caroline
O. Emmerton is this fine old house with
its grounds and gardens connecting the
Hathaway House and the Retire Becket
House, both of the seventeenth century.
It is hard for one to believe, looking at
this quiet harbor now, that after the
Revolution Salem's great fleet of pri-
vateers and prizes taken, opened up a
vast trade with the Far East.

SALEM

THE TOWN HOUSE, DERBY SQUARE. Built in 1816, this was once a market house and is again the scene of a colorful Saturday open market. Here was once the site of the sumptuous mansion of Elias Hasket Derby, designed by Samuel McIntyre and occupied by the owner only a few months. During its demolition much of its carving was incorporated into the Cook-Oliver House on Federal Street.

HAULING OUT FOR THE WINTER. When once the season is over the lovely slim hulls of racing yachts are hauled out and stored at this busy little harbor, where in August craft lie almost as close as fish in a seine. George Norton and a companion from the Cape Ann Colony made the first settlement here and called it Jeffery's Creek.

GLOUCESTER

THE LUMBER SCHOONER "PEACELAND." An occasional three-masted schooner makes port here bringing lumber from the Maine or Canadian woods. But no longer is Gloucester's waterfront a thicket of masts; nor is the town on its slight rise hidden behind a crisscrossing of rigging and spars as in the old days.

The fishing is a very real part of the industrial life of the ports along this rugged coast.

LATE AFTERNOON. It is little wonder that the painter seeks these wharves for action, color, and the play of light on hulls and water. Here, always, is a changeful scene: the out-fitting, loading, or unloading concerned with the fishing—in all weathers and all seasons.

IN THE ITALIAN SECTION. All of the different foreign elements who are concerned with Gloucester's fishing industry add a certain zestful charm to the waterfront.

GLOUCESTER

ALONG THE WHARVES. The tall masts of the square-riggers and the Gloucester schooners have given way to the stubby masts of the diesel-engined trawlers and seiners. Huge industries connected with the fisheries absorb much of the waterfront. The Portuguese section, however, presided over by the Church of the Lady of Good Voyage, retains its own colorful and loquacious identity.

UNLOADING CODFISH. Gloucester has miles of wharves, and many of them now are used by the huge packing industries and their various departments. A Newfoundlander is unloading dried and salted cod at one wharf, while at another under the open sheds, to the lilt of orchestra music from a loud speaker, fish are being graded for their ultimate use.

GLOUCESTER

LITTLE THEATRE, ROCKY NECK. Thrusting out into the inner harbor is the Gloucester School of the Theatre and the Little Theatre, sharing the end of Rocky Neck with a marine railway in an old shipyard.

THE UNIVERSALIST CHURCH. Framed in old trees the front façade of this church rises to a finely proportioned steeple, a copy of the one surmounting an earlier structure of 1774. For centuries it has been a landmark for returning fishermen.

GLOUCESTER

THE ATLANTIC WHARF AND THE GERTRUDE L. THEBAUD. This is the home berth of the famous *Gertrude L. Thebaud*, Gloucester fisherman skippered by the doughty Captain Pine, renowned for the races she has sailed against the Nova Scotians in the Fisherman's International Race. Under racing rig, she is a fast and lovely schooner.

THE COVES OF CAPE ANN. Plum Cove, Lanesville, Folly Cove, and Pigeon Cove are among the earliest outposts of Cape Ann, and are still given over to the very real business of fishing. It was to these fishing hamlets that the colonial farmers came in fall or early winter with country produce to exchange for fresh and salted fish.

CAPE ANN

ROCKPORT "MOTIF NO. 1." Practically every artist fortunate enough to spend a few weeks in Rockport has painted this odd little huddle of fish houses out on the end of one of the huge stone piers. It has been affectionately dubbed "Motif No. 1." Its long granite wharf juts out from Bearskin Neck, that historic site of the old stone fort and the Sea Fencibles Barracks, concerned in action in the War of 1812.

ROCKPORT "MOTIF NO. 2." In quite different values of fading paint on weathered boards, this smaller edition of Motif No. 1 also has its following. Oblivious to the crowding easels, the fishermen go about their business in whatever space on the waterfront is left to them.

ROCKPORT

ROCKPORT SHORELINE. The almost foreign look about this bit of waterfront is part of the charm of the little town that was once called Sandy Bay. It was known for its fine fishing in the days before Pring and Gosnold cruised this coast.

EASTERN POINT LIGHT. Rich in the tradition of the sea that washes its beaches and often piles up in smashing fury on its rocky shore, the Cape continues to live by the element that yields it a precarious living. Its guardian lights such as this, and its attendant Dog Bar Breakwater, built by the Government after the gale of '98, guide and protect the fishing fleet.

The shipyards are full of the activity of building and outfitting ships once more.

LOOKING EAST. It has been said that every vista in this little town has a picture in it for the artist. Its characteristic town shoreline is built up on the huge native granite quays in which Rockport abounds.

FISHING SHACKS. A few of these boathouses, strangely enough the very ones the painters themselves prefer to sketch, resist being made over into studios. However, along Bearskin Neck, running out into Sandy Bay from Dock Square, is a fascinating street of converted fishermen's shacks. It was here, according to the old doggerel, that
*Babson killed the bear
With a knife, I do declare!*

ESSEX *and* IPSWICH

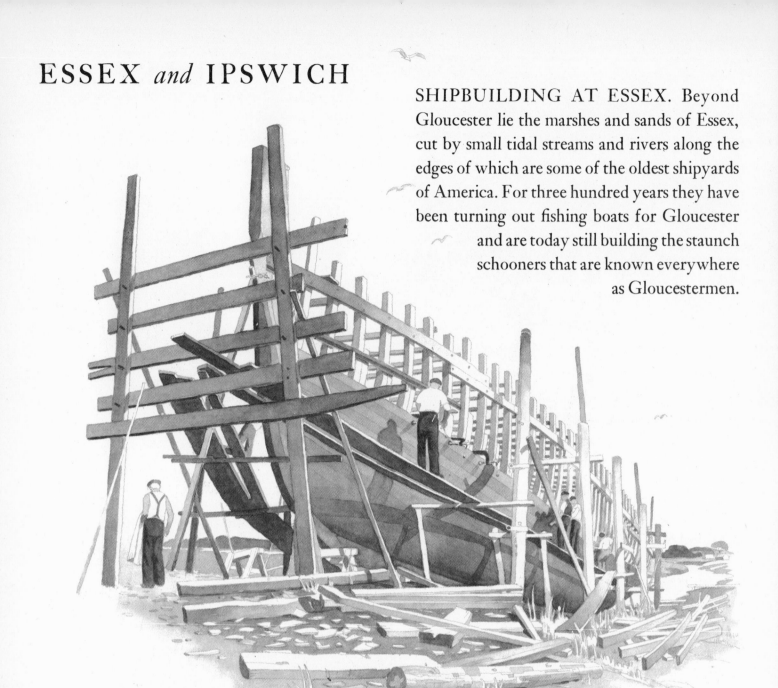

SHIPBUILDING AT ESSEX. Beyond Gloucester lie the marshes and sands of Essex, cut by small tidal streams and rivers along the edges of which are some of the oldest shipyards of America. For three hundred years they have been turning out fishing boats for Gloucester and are today still building the staunch schooners that are known everywhere as Gloucestermen.

THE OLD STONE BRIDGE. One of the earliest settled of Massachusetts towns, Ipswich, formerly known as Agawam, now possesses, besides an attractive long green and several houses of colorful antiquity, a rough-hewn granite bridge of lovely curves, looping across the shallow Ipswich River.

THE TITCOMB HOUSE. Although the fire of 1811 swept through many blocks in the heart of the town, there still stand many of these fine sturdy old early houses carefully preserved. Among the householders all over town the same names persist that once filled the Marine Society roster and the rolls of the Revolutionary Militia.

THE OLD SOUTH CHURCH. This church is now known as the First Presbyterian Meeting House and has been considerably remodeled since George Whitefield, the great English revivalist, came here to preach. He was buried in front of the pulpit, in 1770.

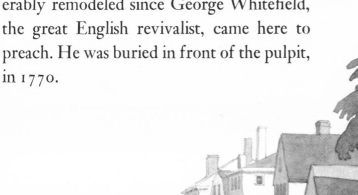

NEWBURYPORT

THE DALTON CLUB. Once the home of Tristram Dalton, this fine gambrel-roofed house built in 1746 has opened its hospitable doors to George Washington and many other notables of the past. The club members still are willing to show its treasures to interested visitors at specified times.

FENCE DETAIL. The carved and curving wooden fences in Newburyport, although not so elaborate or so frequently seen as in Salem, are equally worthy of drawing.

COAL WHARF—SITE OF THE OLD PORTSMOUTH PIER. The exporting of lumber, furs, oil, fish, and other commodities in which this new country was so rich, and the very necessary importing from the old countries, went on the length of Portsmouth's river front in pre-Revolutionary days. It was about here that the old Portsmouth Pier was located, with its rows of merchants' counting houses, warehouses, and shops, for the sale and distribution of those imported comforts and luxuries so dear to the New World.

PORTSMOUTH

STRAWBERRY BANK. In 1631 the settlement that was finally to be known as Portsmouth was called Piscataqua, and then Strawberry Bank, by which diverting name it had been known locally for some time. This part of the river front still retains the old name, and in its old warehouses are the last remnant of the great maritime industry, which so poignantly recall other days.

THE JACKSON HOUSE. The oldest house in Portsmouth is on the Christian Shore across the North Millpond. Since it was put up by John Jackson in 1664, six succeeding generations of Jacksons have occupied it. The Society for the Preservation of New England Antiquities has acquired it and undertaken its restoration.

THE JOHN PAUL JONES HOUSE. Built in 1758 by Captain Gregory Purcell, this house is preserved by the Portsmouth Historical Society. Here it was that John Paul Jones boarded with the widow of this merchant sea captain, when he came to Portsmouth in 1777 to superintend the outfitting of the *Ranger*, recently built on Langdon's Island. It is a comfortable and particularly pleasant old house, and, as a museum, open to visitors.

THE WARNER HOUSE DOORWAY. On the streets of Portsmouth can be found houses that encompass the full span of American architecture from the seventeenth century on. In this fine building, the earliest of brick construction standing, can be read the history of the town, from the time of its erection by Captain Archibbald MacPheadris, a wealthy Scotch merchant, to the present day. It has been preserved by the association formed to restore and care for it. The interior is very interesting, with wall paintings done by an unknown artist who was made the hero of the novel, *Northwest Passage*, by Kenneth Roberts.

PORTSMOUTH

SHEAFE'S WAREHOUSE. Over two hundred years old, this structure was used for storage and unloading gundalows, the shallow and beamy craft peculiar to these waters. They were the river freight boats of the past, carrying loads of salt-meadow hay and market produce up and down the Piscataqua River. The restoration project, concerning itself with the waterfront, has restored this ancient building. It was once owned by Captain Tobias Lear, who aided in the building and outfitting of the *Ranger*, commanded by John Paul Jones.

HOUSES ALONG THE WATERFRONT. From Pleasant Street, once Court, this pleasant gambrel-roofed Oracle House was moved to Haymarket Square and then to the site of the "Great House" on the banks of the river. Here begins part of the restoration of Portsmouth's old waterfront, undertaken by private enterprise for the benefit of the people

THE JACOB WENDELL HOUSE. Purchased in 1815 by Jacob Wendell
from Jeremiah Hill, but dating back to 1789, is this hip-roofed and delightful
home beside Haven Park, bordering on the South Millpond. Its furnishings,
brought from Europe when the house was purchased, have been kept intact by
succeeding generations. It houses a famous collection of Flemish glass.

PORTSMOUTH

ST. JOHN'S CHURCH. Built in 1807 to replace the Queen's Chapel of 1732, destroyed by fire, it contains many historic church relics of the early days of Portsmouth. The bell, taken at Louisburg and recast by Paul Revere, hangs here. The communion silver, given by Queen Caroline, a "Vinegar Bible," and an English-built organ, one of the oldest in the country, "ungodly chest of whistles" as it was called—all are housed in this hilltop church. Many of the tombs of the early parishioners, built into the retaining wall, with ornamental iron doors, open directly on the street.

The sailor home from the sea "swallows the anchor" in seafaring par-
lance and occasionally converts an old warehouse into a curiosity shop.

THE WENTWORTH-GARDNER HOUSE. One of the loveliest of Portsmouth's treasures of the past, and now happily secured unto it forever, this almost perfect example of Georgian architecture stands close to the banks of the Piscataqua. Shaded by the great linden tree planted when the house was new, it has seen the fashions and the manners of the best of Colonial times, the drear years of the Revolution, the upswing of the days of the clipper ships, and then again gradual decline. It was built by Madam Mark Hunking Wentworth as a wedding gift to her son Thomas in 1760, and today is part of the restoration project that has acquired it from the Metropolitan Museum of New York. The project has also acquired the Tobias Lear House from the Society for the Preservation of New England Antiquities.

PORTSMOUTH

GOVERNOR JOHN LANGDON'S HOUSE. In pre-Revolutionary days this town became a seething hive of conflicting Tory and Patriot allegiances. Under the fire of public opinion, veering steadily towards révolution, many Tories fled, including the Royal Governor. Later the Patriot Governor, John Langdon, built this fine house in 1784. He was delegate to the Continental Congress, and first president of the United States Senate. He administered the oath of office to George Washington. Many notable guests, including Washington and Louis Philippe have been entertained here.

THE REVEREND SAMUEL LANGDON HOUSE. This house, built in 1749, bears the name of the Reverend Samuel Langdon, chaplain at Louisburg and later president of Harvard College. It is now the parsonage-home of the minister of the South Unitarian Parish. It has one of the few children's staircases in the country. Within its courtyard are the old stables and sheds surviving from the eighteenth century.

THE MINISTER'S SILVER TANKARD. In the parsonage is a venerable silver tankard, intended by the donor to be used for the minister's own beer and ale. The inscription reads:

The Gift of Mrs. *Mary Shurtleff*
to the Church of the South Parish in Portsmouth
for the use of the MINISTER *thereof*
for the time being

PORTSMOUTH

THE ATHENAEUM. Portsmouth is richer in its surviving domestic architecture than in fine public buildings. But this little gem sandwiched in between business blocks on the Old Parade, or Market Square, sounds a note of beauty worthy of its use. It is the Athenaeum, built in 1803 in the Adam tradition of the Federal period. Now owned by its Proprietors, it is a private repository for portraits, ship models, and a valuable library of 20,000 volumes and original manuscripts. Its lovely main reading room just inside the classic doorway, flanked by cannon taken by Perry at Lake Erie, has been in the past a gathering place for the sea captains of the clipper-ship era.

THE LADY PEPPERELL HOUSE AT KITTERY. The relict of Sir William Pepperell kept up her former pomp and circumstance throughout her widowhood in this house in spite of the shattering effect of the Revolution upon such pretensions. Elaborately Georgian in design, as is the main building, both inside and out, a small room back of the parlor, said to be the work of a local carpenter, is by far the most interesting.

THE BLOCKHOUSE AT FORT McCLARY, KITTERY POINT. The Province of Massachusetts Bay built a fort on this site in 1715. In spite of rebuilding at the time of the Revolution, the War of 1812, and the Civil War, all that remains of interest, aside from the heavy and elaborate hexagonal granite foundations, casemates, and storage cellars, is the old gray granite Blockhouse with its planked overhang, pierced by narrow horizontal slits. Overgrown by wild cherry, sumac, and evergreens, it commands the harbor entrance. It now belongs to the State of Maine.

Marblehead

From the top of Burial Hill the entrancing topography of this little seaport town lies engagingly close with its houses huddled under the shelving rocks so near that their very roof trees could almost be straddled with ease. The horizon far, wide and white with sails, reaches beyond the rocky points that shield a large and a small harbor gay with pleasure craft.